CONTENTS

Look for this panel to see quotes from Pepys' diary.

WHO WAS SAMUEL PEPYS?

Samuel Pepys (say peeps) lived in London in the 17th **century**. It was one of the most **dramatic** times in the history of London.

This portrait of Pepys was painted when he was around thirty years old. Why are there no photographs of Pepys?

Pepys is famous because he wrote a diary for nine years. In his diary, he wrote about everyday life and exciting events. We can learn a lot about life in 17th century London from Pepys' diary.

FACT CAT FACT

Today, you can still buy copies of Pepys' diary.

Pepys saw the Great Fire of London in 1666 (see page 16). He wrote about it in his diary.

EARLY LIFE

Samuel Pepys was born in London in 1633. His parents weren't very rich but some of his **relatives** were wealthy and important. Pepys went to St Paul's School, one of the best schools in London.

Later, Pepys studied at the University of Cambridge.

There was a **civil war** in England in Pepys' childhood. During the war, the king of England, Charles I, was **executed** by his **enemies**.

Crowds of people, including Pepys, watched the execution of King Charles I in 1649. How was Charles I killed?

Pepys was the fifth of eleven children. Sadly, all of his brothers and sisters died when they were children.

WURK AND FAMILY

After Pepys finished university, he worked in the office of his relative, the Earl of Sandwich. The Earl of Sandwich sailed war ships in the British **Navy**. Later, Pepys also worked for the Navy, making sure the ships were ready for battle.

This is a portrait of the Earl of Sandwich. The clothes he is wearing show that he is very wealthy.

In 1655, Pepys got married. His wife's name was Elizabeth. They lived together in a large house in central London.

Pepys and his wife had **servants** to do the housework and cooking. Their servants lived with them.

FACT CAT FACT

Pepys' wife, Elizabeth, was 14 or 15 years old when they got married. Did Pepys and his wife have any children?

THE DIARY

Pepys started writing his diary on 1 January 1660. He wrote in a secret **code** called shorthand so that no one could understand what he had written.

This is the first page from Pepys' diary. Not all of the words are in shorthand.

In Pepys' diary, there is a lot of information about his everyday life. He wrote about his job, his friends and life at home with his wife.

Pepys often wrote about food in his diary. These are some foods that he ate.

cabbage and bacon

lobster

hot chocolate (without sugar)

I had a couple of lobsters and some wine. *30 May 1663*

Most people drank wine or beer with their meals in the 17th century because it was hard to find clean water. What did children drink?

FUN TIMES

From his diary, we know that Pepys often met up with his friends. They ate meals together and went to parties. Pepys liked to go to the theatre to see plays.

Pepys played a musical instrument called the lute. Sometimes he played music and sang with his friends. How do you make music with a lute?

FACT CAT FACT

Before the 17th century, women didn't act in plays. Women's parts were played by men dressed as women. Pepys saw a woman in a play for the first time on 3 January 1661.

Rich people, such as Pepys and his friends, wore fancy clothes to show that they were important. Some men, including Pepys, covered their hair with **wigs** made from real human hair.

Tailors made clothes by hand for rich people. Poor people made their own clothes.

This day I put on my new silk suit, the first that ever I wore in my life.
10 July 1660

THE PLAGUE

In the spring of 1665, many people in London became sick with a disease called the **plague**. Pepys lived in London at that time. He wrote about the plague in his diary.

This picture shows a man suffering from the plague. People with the plague had large bumps all over their bodies.

The town grows very sickly and people are afraid of it.
15 June 1665

Some people moved to towns outside of London so that they wouldn't catch the plague. Many of the people who stayed in the city died from the plague. Their bodies were **buried** in the countryside.

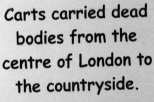

Carts carried dead bodies from the centre of London to the countryside.

This is a drawing of a doctor who treated people with the plague. Plague doctors wore special masks and clothes that they thought would stop them from catching the plague.

FIRE IN LONDON

On 2 September 1666, a fire started in a bakery on Pudding Lane, in central London. The wooden buildings around the bakery quickly caught fire. This was the beginning of the Great Fire of London.

Pepys wrote in his diary about how a strong wind **spread** the fire across London. Did the fire spread to the other side of the river?

The churches, houses, and all on fire and flaming at once.
2 September 1666

Pepys **advised** King Charles II about the fire. He told the king that buildings should be pulled down because the fire couldn't move across gaps in the streets. Pepys' idea helped to slow down the fire.

Some people tried to put out the fire with the only equipment they had – **water squirts** and buckets of water.

water squirt

FACT CAT FACT

King Charles II and his brother, James, helped to throw water on the fire!

THE END OF THE FIRE

Many homes and **possessions** were **destroyed** in the fire. Pepys was worried that his house would catch fire so he left his money and **valuable** possessions at a friend's house.

Some people left London to **escape** the fire. They carried their possessions in bags. How many people died in the Great Fire of London?

On 6 September, the Great Fire of London ended. It took many years to rebuild London after the fire. The new buildings were made from stone so that they couldn't catch fire again.

St Paul's Cathedral was rebuilt after it burned down in the fire.

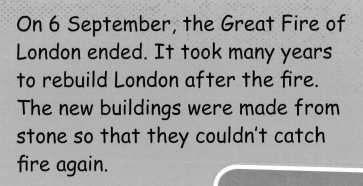

FACT CAT FACT

Pepys buried a large cheese and bottles of wine in his garden to keep them safe from the fire!

LATER YEARS

In 1673, Pepys became a **Member of Parliament**. He also had a good job in the Navy. Pepys' enemies were angry that he was so important. They said that he was a spy who had given away important secrets about the English Navy, but this wasn't true.

In 1679, Pepys was sent to prison in the Tower of London for several months. Is the Tower of London a prison today?

FACT CAT FACT

In 1669, Pepys stopped writing his diary. His eyesight was very bad and he was worried that writing in his diary might make him go **blind**.

Towards the end of his life, Pepys collected books. When he died in 1703, he left his diary and his collection of more than 3,000 books to the University of Cambridge.

Today, people around the world remember Pepys for his diary.

QUIZ

Try to answer the questions below. Look back through the book to help you. Check your answers on page 24.

1 For how many years did Pepys write his diary?

a) five
b) nine
c) twelve

2 Pepys had two brothers and sisters. True or not true?

a) true
b) not true

3 What was the name of Pepys' wife?

a) Elizabeth
b) Sarah
c) Catherine

4 Pepys wore a wig made from real hair. True or not true?

a) true
b) not true

5 In which year was the Great Fire of London?

a) 1660
b) 1665
c) 1666

6 Pepys stopped writing in his diary because he was sent to prison. True or not true?

a) true
b) not true

GLOSSARY

advise to give someone advice

blind describes someone who can't see

bury to put something in a hole in the ground and cover it with soil

century a period of 100 years. The 17th century refers to dates between 1600 and 1699.

civil war a war between groups of people who live in the same country

code a way of writing that keeps the message secret

destroyed when something is damaged so badly that it doesn't exist any more

dramatic describes something that is full of action and excitement

enemy a person who doesn't like another person and tries to make their life difficult

escape to get away from a place where you do not want to be

execute to be killed as a punishment

Member of Parliament a person who is chosen to make the laws of a country

Navy the group of ships and sailors who fight wars at sea

plague a terrible disease that killed lots of people in the past

possession an object that you own

relative a member of your family

servant someone who lives and works in another person's house doing cooking and cleaning

spread to move over a larger area

tailor someone whose job it is to make clothes

valuable describes something that is worth a lot of money

water squirt a machine that was used to squirt water at a fire during the Great Fire of London

wig something that covers your head, made from real or fake hair

INDEX

ANSWERS

Pages 4–20

page 4: Because photography had not been invented when Pepys was alive.

page 7: His head was chopped off.

page 9: No, they didn't.

page 11: Children also drank beer or wine.

page 12: You play the lute by plucking the strings with your fingers, similar to a guitar.

page 14: No, you cannot catch the plague in London today. However, people still catch the plague in some parts of the world today.

page 16: No, the fire stayed on the north side of the river.

page 18: According to official records, fewer than ten people died in the Great Fire of London.

page 20: No, the Tower of London is a museum today.

Quiz answers

1 b - nine

2 not true – he had ten brothers and sisters.

3 a - Elizabeth

4 true

5 c - 1666

6 not true – he stopped because he was worried about his eyesight.